from

THE BASIC LAWS OF HUMAN STUPIDITY

Law #1: Always and inevitably everyone underestimates the number of stupid individuals in circulation.

·

Law #2: The probability that a certain person be stupid is independent of any other characteristic of that person.

·

Law #3: A stupid person is a person who causes losses to another person or to a group of persons while himself deriving no gain and even possibly incurring losses.

·

Law #4: Non-stupid people always underestimate the damaging power of stupid individuals. In particular non-stupid people constantly forget that at all times and places and under any circumstances to deal and/or associate with stupid people infallibly turns out to be a costly mistake.

·

Law #5: A stupid person is the most dangerous type of person. A stupid person is more dangerous than a bandit.

THE
BASIC
LAWS OF
HUMAN
STUPIDITY

CARLO M. CIPOLLA

FOREWORD BY

NASSIM NICHOLAS TALEB

DOUBLEDAY ⚓ NEW YORK

www.doubleday.com

Jacket photograph by CribbVisuals / E+ / Getty Images
Jacket design by John Fontana

Library of Congress Cataloging-in-Publication Data
Names: Cipolla, Carlo M., author. | Taleb, Nassim
Nicholas, [date]- writer of foreword.
Title: The basic laws of human stupidity / Carlo M. Cipolla ;
with a foreword by Nassim Nicholas Taleb.
Other titles: Leggi fondamentali della stupidità umana. English.
Description: London : WH Allen, 2019. | "The Basic Laws of Human
Stupidity was originally published in Italian in 1988 by Società
editrice il Mulino. First published in English by Società editrice
il Mulino. © 2011 by Società editrice il Mulino, Bologna."
Identifiers: LCCN 2019047891 (print) | LCCN 2019047892 (ebook) |
ISBN 9780385546478 (hardcover) | ISBN 9780385546485 (ebook)
Subjects: LCSH: Stupidity—Humor. | Conduct of life—Humor.
Classification: LCC PN6231.S77 C5713 2019 (print) |
LCC PN6231.S77 (ebook) | DDC 857/.92—dc23
LC record available at https://lccn.loc.gov/2019047891
LC ebook record available at https://lccn.loc.gov/2019047892

MANUFACTURED IN CANADA

3 5 7 9 10 8 6 4

First American Edition

CONTENTS

Foreword by Nassim Nicholas Taleb   *vii*

Publisher's Note   *xi*

The Mad Millers to the Reader   *xiii*

Introduction   1

   I.   The First Basic Law   5

   II.   The Second Basic Law   11

  III.   A Technical Interlude   21

  IV.   The Third (and Golden) Basic Law   29

   V.   Frequency Distribution   37

  VI.   Stupidity and Power   45

  VII.   The Power of Stupidity   51

VIII.   The Fourth Basic Law   57

  IX.   Macro Analysis and the Fifth Basic Law   65

Appendix   75

FOREWORD
NASSIM NICHOLAS TALEB

When I start at the top left corner of a page in *The Basic Laws of Human Stupidity*, I have the feeling of reading a satire. Ten lines into it, some doubts erupt—could this be serious? When I reach the bottom right corner, I am certain it must be a serious work of scholarship in economic analysis. Then, upon turning the page, the cycle starts again, thankfully, because economics is boring (by design) and this is playful, hence fun to read.

The Basic Laws asserts that 1) there will always be more stupid people than you think; 2) the proportion of stupid people is invariant to intellectual, social or geographic segmentation. The ratio will be the same among Nobel Prize winners as it will be among a selection of tax accountants (except I am sure that there must be a higher prevalence among laureates of the pseudo-Nobel in economics). I will leave the remaining laws to avoid spoiling the read—this is a very short book.

By the time my eyes reach the bottom right corner, and I realize this is not a joke, the following ideas pop into my head. First, the author has a formal *axiomatic* definition of what stupid means: someone who harms others without procuring any gain for himself or herself—in contrast to the much more predictable bandit who gains something from harming you. As such, stupid persons can cause a lot of damage—unlike bandits, they have no interest in the survival of the system because they do not benefit from their stupidity. Second, the *laws* here are real laws, as far as economic laws are concerned, no less rigorously obtained than Adam Smith's three laws, the law of diminishing return, Okun's law, or some such thing you forget about seconds after taking the final exam. (By contrast, I promise that you will remember Cipolla's laws forever.)

Finally, one wonders: Why is there a constant

proportion of stupid people, invariant to time, place, geography, profession, body mass index, degrees of separation from the Queen of Denmark and professional rank? The solution to the mystery may lie in the Italian title of Cipolla's work, *Allegro ma non troppo*. Fast, but not too fast. Could it be that Mother Nature (or God, whatever your theology) wants to put a brake on things, reduce the speed of progress, slow down the growth of your employer, prevent GDP from an exponential rise so the economy doesn't overheat? So *She* created the stupid person acting against both his and the collective interest to do just that?

A masterly book.

PUBLISHER'S NOTE

Originally written in English, *The Basic Laws of Human Stupidity* was published for the first time in 1976 in a numbered and private edition bearing the unlikely imprint of "Mad Millers."

The author believed that his short essay could be fully appreciated only in the language in which it had been written. He consequently long declined any proposal to have it translated. Only in 1988 did he accept the idea of its publication in an Italian version as part of the volume titled *Allegro ma non troppo,* together with the essay *Pepper, Wine (and Wool) as the Dynamic Factors of the Social and Economic Development of the Middle Ages,* also originally written in English and published privately by Mad Millers for Christmas 1973.

Allegro ma non troppo has been a bestseller both in Italy and in all the countries where translated versions have appeared. Yet, with an irony that the author of these laws would have appreciated, it has never been published in the language in which it was first written.

Thus, more than a quarter of a century since the publication of *Allegro ma non troppo,* this in fact is the first edition that makes *The Basic Laws of Human Stupidity* available in its original version.

THE MAD MILLERS
TO THE READER

The private edition of 1976 was preceded by the following publisher's note written by the author himself:

The Mad Millers printed only a limited number of copies of this book, which addresses itself not to stupid people but to those who on occasion have to deal with such people. To add that none of those who will receive this book can possibly fall in area S of the basic graph (figure 1) is therefore a work of supererogation. Nevertheless, like most works of supererogation, it is better done than left undone. For, as the Chinese philosopher said: "Erudition is the source of universal wisdom: but that does not prevent it from being an occasional cause of misunderstanding between friends."

INTRODUCTION

Human affairs are admittedly in a deplorable state. This, however, is no novelty. As far back as we can see, human affairs have always been in a deplorable state. The heavy load of troubles and miseries that human beings have to bear as individuals as well as members of organized societies is basically a by-product of the most improbable—and I would dare say, stupid—way in which life was set up at its very inception.

After Darwin, we know that we share our origin with the lower members of the animal kingdom, and worms as well as elephants have to bear their daily share of trials, predicaments, and ordeals. Human beings, however, are privileged insofar as they have to bear an extra load—an extra dose of tribulations originated daily by a group of people within the human race itself. This group is much more powerful than the Mafia, or the military industrial complex, or international communism—it is an unorganized, unchartered group which has no chief, no president, no by-laws and yet manages to operate in perfect unison, as if guided by an invisible hand, in such a way that the activity of each member powerfully contributes to strengthen and amplify the effectiveness of the activity of all other members. The nature, character, and behavior of the members of this group are the subject of the following pages.

Let me point out at this juncture that most emphatically this little book is neither a product of cynicism nor an exercise in defeatism—no more than a book on microbiology is. The following pages are in fact the result of a constructive effort to detect, know, and thus possibly neutralize one of the most powerful dark forces that hinder the growth of human welfare and happiness.

CHAPTER I

THE FIRST BASIC LAW

ALWAYS AND
INEVITABLY
EVERYONE
UNDERESTIMATES

THE NUMBER
OF STUPID
INDIVIDUALS IN
CIRCULATION.

The First Basic Law of Human Stupidity asserts without ambiguity that

Always and inevitably everyone underestimates the number of stupid individuals in circulation.*

At first, the statement sounds trivial, vague and horribly ungenerous. Closer scrutiny will, however, reveal its realistic veracity. No matter how high are

---

* The compilers of the Testament were aware of the First Basic Law, and they paraphrased it when they asserted that *"stultorum infinitus est numerus,"* but they indulged in poetic exaggeration. The number of stupid people cannot be infinite because the number of living people is finite.

one's estimates of human stupidity, one is repeatedly and recurrently startled by the fact that

a) people whom one had once judged rational and intelligent turn out to be unashamedly stupid;

b) day after day, with unceasing monotony, one is harassed in one's activities by stupid individuals who appear suddenly and unexpectedly in the most inconvenient places and at the most improbable moments.

The First Basic Law prevents me from attributing a specific numerical value to the fraction of stupid people within the total population: any numerical estimate would turn out to be an underestimate. Thus in the following pages I will denote the fraction of stupid people within a population by the symbol σ.

CHAPTER II

THE SECOND BASIC LAW

THE PROBABILITY
THAT A CERTAIN
PERSON BE STUPID

IS INDEPENDENT
OF ANY OTHER
CHARACTERISTIC OF
THAT PERSON.

Cultural trends now fashionable in the West favor an egalitarian approach to life. People like to think of human beings as the output of a perfectly engineered mass production machine. Geneticists and sociologists especially go out of their way to prove, with an impressive apparatus of scientific data and formulations, that all men are naturally equal and if some are more equal than the others, this is attributable to nurture and not to nature.

I take exception to this general view. It is my firm conviction, supported by years of observation and experimentation, that men are not equal, that some are stupid and others are not and that the difference is determined by nature and not by cultural forces or factors. One is stupid in the same way one is red-haired; one belongs to the stupid set as one belongs to a blood group. A stupid man is born a stupid man by an act of Providence.

Although convinced that fraction σ of human beings are stupid and that they are so because of genetic traits, I am not a reactionary trying to reintroduce surreptitiously class or race discrimination. I firmly believe that stupidity is an indiscriminate privilege of all human groups and is uniformly distributed according to a constant proportion. This fact is scientifically expressed by the Second Basic Law, which states that

The probability that a certain person be stupid is independent of any other characteristic of that person.

In this regard, Nature seems indeed to have outdone herself. It is well known that Nature manages, rather mysteriously, to keep constant the relative frequency of certain natural phenomena.

For instance, whether men proliferate at the North Pole or at the equator, whether the matching couples are developed or developing, whether they are black or white, the female to male ratio among the newly born is a constant, with a very slight prevalence of males. We do not know how Nature achieves this remarkable result but we know that in order to achieve it Nature must operate with large numbers. The most remarkable fact about the frequency of stupidity is that Nature succeeds in making this frequency equal to the probability σ quite independently from the size of the group. Thus one finds the same percentage of stupid people whether one is considering very large groups or dealing with very small ones. No other set of observable phenomena offers such striking proof of the powers of Nature.

The evidence that education has nothing to do with the probability σ was provided by experiments carried out in a large number of universities all over the world. One may distinguish the composite population that constitutes a university in five major groups, namely the blue-collar workers, the white-collar employees, the students, the administrators, and the professors.

Whenever I analyzed the blue-collar workers I found that the fraction σ of them were stupid. As σ's value was higher than I expected (First Law), paying my tribute to fashion I thought at first that segregation, poverty, lack of education were to be blamed. But moving up the social ladder I found that the same ratio was prevalent among the white-collar employees and among the students. More impressive still were the results among the professors. Whether I considered a large university or a small college, a famous institution or an obscure one, I found that the same fraction σ of the professors were stupid. So bewildered was I by the results that I made a special point to extend my research to a specially selected group, to a real elite, the Nobel laureates. The result confirmed Nature's supreme powers: σ fraction of the Nobel laureates were stupid.

This idea was hard to accept and digest, but too many experimental results proved its fundamental veracity. The Second Basic Law is an iron law, and it does not admit exceptions. The Women's Liberation Movement will support the Second Basic Law; as it shows that stupid individuals are proportionally as numerous among men as among women. The "developing" of the "Third World" will probably take solace in the Second Basic Law as they can find in it the proof that after all the developed are not so developed. Whether the Second Basic Law is liked or not, however, its implications are frightening: the law implies that whether you move in distinguished circles or you take refuge among the headhunters of Polynesia, whether you lock yourself in a monastery or decide to spend the rest of your life in the company of beautiful and lascivious women, you always have to face the same percentage of stupid people—which percentage (in accordance with the First Law) will always surpass your expectations.

CHAPTER III

A
TECHNICAL
INTERLUDE

At this point it is imperative to elucidate the concept of human stupidity and to define the dramatis personae.

Individuals are characterized by different degrees of propensity to socialize. There are individuals for whom any contact with other individuals is a painful necessity. They literally have to put up with people, and people have to put up with them. At the other extreme of the spectrum there are individuals who absolutely cannot live by themselves and are even ready to spend time in the company of people whom they do not really like rather than be alone. Between these two extremes, there is an extreme variety of conditions, although by far the greatest majority of people are closer to the type who cannot face loneliness than to the type who has no taste for human intercourse. Aristotle recognized this fact when he wrote that "Man is a social animal" and the validity of his statement is demonstrated by the fact that we move in social groups, that there are more married people than bachelors and spinsters, that so much wealth and time are wasted in fatiguing and boring cocktail parties, and that the word *loneliness* normally carries a negative connotation.

Whether one belongs to the hermit or to the socialite type, one deals with people, although with different intensity. Even the hermits occasionally meet people. Moreover, one affects human beings also by avoiding them. What I could have done for an individual or a group but did not do is an opportunity-cost (i.e., a lost gain or loss) for that particular person or group. The moral of the story is that each one of us has a current balance with everybody else. From each action or inaction we derive a gain or a loss and at the same time we cause a gain or a loss to someone else. Gains and losses can be

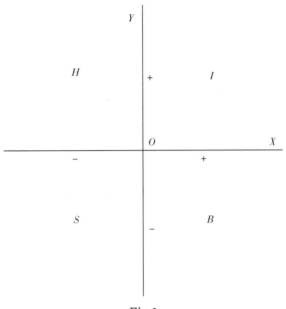

Fig. 1

conveniently charted on a graph, and figure 1 shows the basic graph to be used for the purpose.

The graph refers to an individual—let us say Tom. The X-axis measures the gain that Tom derives from his actions. On the Y-axis the graph shows the gain that another person or group of persons derives from Tom's actions. Gains can be positive, nil, or negative—a negative gain being actually a loss. The *X*-axis measures Tom's positive gains to the right of point *O* and Tom's losses to the left of point *O*. The *Y*-axis measures the gains and losses of the person or persons with whom Tom deals respectively above and below point *O*.

To make all this clear, let us use a hypothetical example and refer to figure 1. Tom takes an action that affects Dick. If Tom derives from the action a gain and Dick suffers from the same action a loss, the action will be recorded on the graph with a dot that will appear in the graph somewhere in area *B*.

Gains and losses may be recorded on the *X*- and *Y*-axis in dollars or francs, if one wants, but one has to include also psychological and emotional rewards and satisfactions as well as psychological and emotional stresses. These are intangibles and they are very difficult to measure according to objective standards. Cost-benefit analysis can help to solve the problem, although not completely, but I do not want to bother the reader with such technicalities:

a margin of imprecision is bound to affect the measurement but it does not affect the essence of the argument. One point though must be made clear. When considering Tom's action one makes use of Tom's values but one has to rely on Dick's values and not on Tom's values to determine Dick's gains (whether positive or negative). All too often this rule of fairness is forgotten, and many troubles originate from failure to apply this essentially urbane point of view. Let me resort once again to a banal example. Tom hits Dick on Dick's head and he derives satisfaction from his action. He may pretend that Dick was delighted to be hit on the head. Dick, however, may not share Tom's view. In fact he may regard the blow to his head as an unpleasant event. Whether the blow to Dick's head was a gain or a loss to Dick is up to Dick to decide and not to Tom.

CHAPTER IV

THE THIRD (AND GOLDEN) BASIC LAW

A STUPID PERSON
IS A PERSON WHO
CAUSES LOSSES TO
ANOTHER PERSON
OR TO A GROUP
OF PERSONS

WHILE HIMSELF
DERIVING NO GAIN
AND EVEN POSSIBLY
INCURRING LOSSES.

The Third Basic Law assumes, although it does not state it explicitly, that human beings fall into four basic categories: the helpless, the intelligent, the bandit, and the stupid. It will be easily recognized by the perspicacious reader that these four categories correspond to the four areas H, I, B, S of the basic graph (see figure 1).

If Tom takes an action and suffers a loss while producing a gain to Dick, Tom's mark will fall in field H: Tom acted helplessly. If Tom takes an action by which he makes a gain while yielding a gain also to Dick, Tom's mark will fall in area I: Tom acted intelligently. If Tom takes an action by which he makes a gain causing Dick a loss, Tom's mark will fall in area *B*: Tom acted as a bandit. Stupidity is related to area *S* and to all positions on *Y*-axis below point *O*.

As the Third Basic Law explicitly clarifies:

A stupid person is a person who causes losses to another person or to a group of persons while himself deriving no gain and even possibly incurring losses.

When confronted for the first time with the Third Basic Law, rational people instinctively react with feelings of skepticism and incredulousness. The fact is that reasonable people have difficulty conceiving and understanding unreasonable behavior. But let us abandon the lofty plane of theory and let us look pragmatically at our daily life. We all recollect occasions in which a fellow took an action that resulted in his gain and in our loss: we had to deal with a bandit. We also recollect cases in which a fellow took an action that resulted in his loss and in our gain:

we had to deal with a helpless person.* We can recollect cases in which a fellow took an action by which both parties gained: he was intelligent. Such cases do indeed occur. But upon thoughtful reflection you must admit that these are not the events that punctuate most frequently our daily life. Our daily life is mostly made up of cases in which we lose money and/or time and/or energy and/or appetite, cheerfulness, and good health because of the improbable action of some preposterous creature who has nothing to gain and indeed gains nothing from causing us embarrassment, difficulties or harm. Nobody knows, understands, or can possibly explain why that preposterous creature does what he does. In fact there is no explanation—or better, there is only one explanation: the person in question is stupid.

---

* Notice the qualification "a fellow *took* an action." The fact *he* took the action is decisive in establishing that he is helpless. If *I* took the action which resulted in my gain and his loss, then the judgment would be different: *I* would be a bandit.

CHAPTER V

FREQUENCY DISTRIBUTION

Most people do not act consistently. Under certain circumstances a given person acts intelligently and under different circumstances the same person will act helplessly. The only important exception to the rule is represented by the stupid people, who normally show a strong proclivity toward perfect consistency in all fields of human endeavors.

From all that proceeds, it does not follow that we can chart on the basic graph only stupid individuals. We can calculate for each person his weighted average position in the plane of figure 1 quite independently from his degree of inconsistency. A helpless person may occasionally behave intelligently and on occasion he may perform a bandit's action. But since the person in question is fundamentally helpless, most of his action will have the characteristics of helplessness. Thus the overall weighted average position of all the actions of such a person will place him in the H quadrant of the basic graph.

The fact that it is possible to place on the graph individuals instead of their actions allows some variance in the frequency of the bandit and stupid types.

The perfect bandit is one who, with his actions, causes to other individuals losses equal to his gains. The crudest type of banditry is theft. A person who robs you of 100 dollars without causing you an extra loss or harm is a perfect bandit: you lose 100 dollars, he gains 100 pounds. In the basic graph the perfect bandits would appear on a 45-degree diagonal line that divides the area B into two perfectly symmetrical subareas (line OM of figure 2).

However, the "perfect" bandits are relatively few. The line OM divides the area B into two subareas, B_I and B_S, and by far the largest majority of the bandits fall somewhere in one of these two subareas.

The bandits who fall in area B_I are those individuals whose actions yield to them profits that are

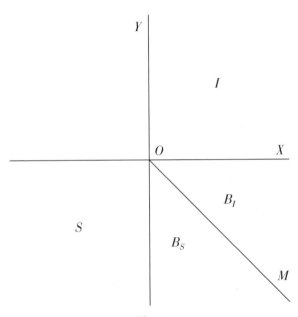

Fig. 2

larger than the losses they cause to other people. All bandits who are entitled to a position in area B_I are bandits with overtones of intelligence, and as they get closer to the right side of the X-axis they share more and more the characteristics of the intelligent person. Unfortunately the individuals entitled to a position in the B_I area are not very numerous. Most bandits actually fall in area B_S. The individuals who fall in this area are those whose actions yield to them gains inferior to the losses inflicted to other people. If someone kills you in order to rob you of fifty dollars or if he murders you in order to spend a weekend with your wife at Monte Carlo, we can be sure that he is not a perfect bandit. Even by using *his* values to measure *his* gains (but still using *your* values to measure *your* losses), he falls in the B_S area very close to the border of sheer stupidity. Generals who cause vast destruction and innumerable casualties in return for a promotion or a medal fall in the same area.

The frequency distribution of the stupid people is totally different from that of the bandit. While bandits are mostly scattered over an area, stupid people are heavily concentrated along one line, specifically on the Y-axis below point O. The reason for this is that by far the majority of stupid people are basically and unwaveringly stupid—in other words they perseveringly insist on causing harm and losses to other people without deriving any gain, whether positive or negative. There are, however, people who by their improbable actions not only cause damage to other people but in addition hurt themselves. They are a sort of super-stupid who, in our system of accounting, will appear somewhere in the area S to the left of the Y-axis.

CHAPTER VI

STUPIDITY AND POWER

Like all human creatures, stupid people vary enormously in their capacity to affect their fellow men. Some stupid people normally cause only limited losses while others egregiously succeed in causing ghastly and widespread damage not only to one or two individuals but to entire communities or societies. The damaging potential of the stupid person depends on two major factors. First of all, it depends on the genetic factor. Some individuals inherit exceptional doses of the gene of stupidity and by virtue of inheritance they belong from birth to the elite of their group. The second factor that determines the potential of a stupid person is related to the position of power and consequence that he occupies in society. Among bureaucrats, generals, politicians, and heads of state one has little difficulty in finding clear examples of basically stupid individuals whose damaging capacity was (or is) alarmingly enhanced by the position of power that they occupied (or occupy). Religious dignitaries should not be overlooked.

The question that reasonable people often raise is how and why stupid people can reach positions of power and consequence.

Class and caste were the social arrangements that favored the steady supply of stupid people to positions of power in most societies of the preindustrial world. Religion was another contributing factor. In the modern industrial world, class and caste are banished, both as words and as concepts, and religion is fading away. But in lieu of class and caste we have political parties and bureaucracy, and in lieu of religion we have democracy. Within a democratic system, general elections are a most effective instrument to ensure the steady maintenance of fraction σ among the powerful. One has to keep in mind that according to the Second Basic Law, the fraction σ of the voting population are stupid people and elections offer to all of them at once a magnificent opportunity to harm everybody else without gaining anything from their action. They do so by contributing to the maintenance of the σ level among those in power.

CHAPTER VII

THE POWER OF STUPIDITY

It is not difficult to understand how social, political, and institutional power enhances the damaging potential of a stupid person. But one still has to explain and understand what essentially it is that makes a stupid person dangerous to other people—in other words what constitutes the power of stupidity.

Essentially, stupid people are dangerous and damaging because reasonable people find it difficult to imagine and understand unreasonable behavior. An intelligent person may understand the logic of a bandit. The bandit's actions follow a pattern of rationality: nasty rationality, if you like, but still rationality. The bandit wants a plus on his account. Since he is not intelligent enough to devise ways of obtaining the plus as well as providing you with a plus, he will produce his plus by causing a minus to appear on your account. All this is bad, but it is rational and if you are rational you can predict it. You can foresee a bandit's actions, his nasty maneuvers, and ugly aspirations, and often can build up your defenses.

With a stupid person all this is absolutely impossible, as explained by the Third Basic Law. A stupid creature will harass you for no reason, for no advantage, without any plan or scheme and at the most improbable times and places. You have no rational way of telling if and when and how and why the stupid creature attacks. When confronted with a stupid individual you are completely at his mercy.

Because the stupid person's actions do not conform to the rules of rationality, it follows that

a) one is generally caught by surprise by the attack;

b) even when one becomes aware of the attack, one cannot organize a rational defense, because the attack itself lacks any rational structure.

The fact that the activity and movements of a stupid creature are absolutely erratic and irrational not only makes defense problematic but it also makes any counterattack extremely difficult—like trying to shoot at an object that is capable of the most improbable and unimaginable movements. This is what both Dickens and Schiller had in mind when the former stated that "with stupidity and sound digestion man may front much" and the latter wrote that "against stupidity the very Gods fight in vain."

CHAPTER VIII

THE FOURTH BASIC LAW

NON-STUPID
PEOPLE ALWAYS
UNDERESTIMATE THE
DAMAGING POWER OF
STUPID INDIVIDUALS.

IN PARTICULAR
NON-STUPID PEOPLE
CONSTANTLY
FORGET THAT AT ALL
TIMES AND PLACES
AND UNDER ANY
CIRCUMSTANCES
TO DEAL AND/OR
ASSOCIATE WITH
STUPID PEOPLE
INFALLIBLY TURNS
OUT TO BE A COSTLY
MISTAKE.

That helpless people, namely those who in our accounting system fall into the *H* area, do not normally recognize how dangerous stupid people are is not at all surprising. Their failure is just another expression of their helplessness. The truly amazing fact, however, is that intelligent people and bandits also often fail to recognize the power to damage inherent in stupidity. It is extremely difficult to explain why this should happen, and one can only remark that when confronted with stupid individuals, intelligent men as well as bandits often make the mistake of indulging in feelings of self-complacency and contemptuousness instead of immediately secreting adequate quantities of adrenaline and building up defenses.

One is tempted to believe that a stupid man will do harm only to himself, but this is confusing stupidity with helplessness. On occasion one is tempted to associate oneself with a stupid individual in order to use him for one's own schemes. Such a maneuver can only have disastrous effects because

a) it is based on a complete misunderstanding of the essential nature of stupidity;

b) it gives the stupid person added scope for the exercise of his gifts.

One may hope to outmaneuver the stupid and up to a point one may actually do so. But because of the erratic behavior of the stupid, one cannot foresee all the stupid's actions and reactions, and before long one will be pulverized by the unpredictable moves of the stupid partner.

This is clearly summarized in the Fourth Basic Law, which states that

Non-stupid people always underestimate the damaging power of stupid individuals. In particular non-stupid people constantly

forget that at all times and places and under any circumstances to deal and/ or associate with stupid people infallibly turns out to be a costly mistake.

Through centuries and millennia, in public as in private life, countless individuals have failed to take account of the Fourth Basic Law, and the failure has caused mankind incalculable losses.

CHAPTER IX

MACRO ANALYSIS AND THE FIFTH BASIC LAW

A STUPID PERSON
IS THE MOST
DANGEROUS TYPE OF
PERSON.

A STUPID PERSON IS
MORE DANGEROUS
THAN A BANDIT.

The consideration on which the previous chapter ends is conducive to a macro-type analysis in which instead of considering the welfare of the individual one considers the welfare of the society, regarded in this context as the algebraic sum of the individual conditions. A full understanding of the Fifth Basic Law is essential to the analysis. It may be parenthetically added here that of the Five Basic Laws, the fifth is certainly the best known and its corollary is quoted very frequently. The Fifth Basic Law states that

A stupid person is the most dangerous type of person.

The corollary of the law is

**A stupid person is more
dangerous than a bandit.**

The formulation of the law and its corollary is still of the micro-type. As indicated above, however, the law and its corollary have far-reaching implications of a macro-nature.

The essential point to keep in mind is this: the result of the action of a perfect bandit (the person who falls on line OM of figure 2) is purely and simply a transfer of wealth and/or welfare. After the action of a perfect bandit, the bandit has a plus on his account that is exactly equivalent to the minus he has caused to another person. The society as a whole is neither better nor worse off. If all members of a society were perfect bandits the society would remain stagnant but there would be no major disaster. The whole business would amount to massive transfers of wealth and welfare in favor of those who would take action. If all members of the society would take action in regular turns, not only the society as a whole but also individuals would find themselves in a perfectly steady state of no change.

When stupid people are at work, the story is totally different. Stupid people cause losses to other people with no counterpart of gains on their own account. Thus the society as a whole is impoverished.

The system of accounting that finds expression in the basic graphs shows that while all actions of individuals falling to the right of the line *POM* (see figure 3) add to the welfare of a society, although to different degrees, the actions of all individuals falling to the left of the same line *POM* cause a deterioration.

In other words the helpless with overtones of intelligence (area H_I), the bandits with overtones of intelligence (area B_I) and above all the intelligent (area I) all contribute, though in different degrees, to accrue to the welfare of a society. On the other hand, the bandits with overtones of stupidity (area B_S) and the helpless with overtones of stupidity (area H_S) manage to add losses to those caused by

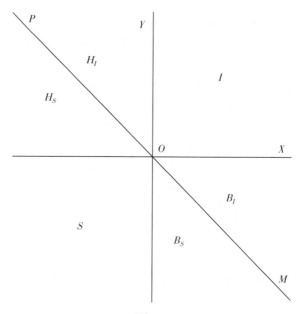

Fig. 3

stupid people thus enhancing the nefarious destructive power of the latter group.

All this suggests some reflection on the perfor-
mance of societies. According to the Second Basic
Law, the fraction of stupid people is a constant σ,
which is not affected by time, space, race, class, or

any other sociocultural or historical variable. It would be a profound mistake to believe the number of stupid people in a declining society is greater than in a developing society. Both such societies are plagued by the same percentage of stupid people. The difference between the two societies is that in the society that performs poorly

a) the stupid members of the society are allowed by the other members to become more active and take more actions;

b) there is a change in the composition of the non-stupid section with a relative decline of populations of areas I, H_I and B_I and a proportionate increase of populations of areas H_S and B_S.

This theoretical presumption is abundantly confirmed by an exhaustive analysis of historical cases. In fact, the historical analysis allows us to reformulate the theoretical conclusions in a more factual way and with more realistic detail.

Whether one considers classical, or medieval, or modern, or contemporary times, one is impressed by the fact that any country moving uphill has its unavoidable σ fraction of stupid people. However, the country moving uphill also has an unusually high fraction of intelligent people who manage to keep the σ fraction at bay and at the same time produce enough gains for themselves and the other members of the community to make progress a certainty.

In a country that is moving downhill, the fraction of stupid people is still equal to σ; however, in the remaining population one notices among those in power an alarming proliferation of the bandits with overtones of stupidity (subarea B_S of quadrant B in figure 3) and among those not in power an equally alarming growth in the number of helpless individuals (area H in the basic graph, figure 1). Such change in the composition of the non-stupid population inevitably strengthens the destructive power of the σ fraction and makes decline a certainty. And the country goes to Hell.

APPENDIX

In the following pages the reader will find a number of basic graphs, which he can use to record the actions of individuals or groups with whom he is currently dealing. This will enable the reader to produce useful evaluations of the individuals or groups under scrutiny and will allow him to take a rational course of action.

NAMES

X = ...

Y = (The reader)

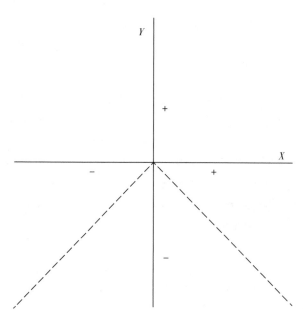

NAMES

X = ...

Y = (The reader)

NAMES

X = ...

Y = (The reader)

NAMES

$X =$ ....

$Y =$ (The reader)

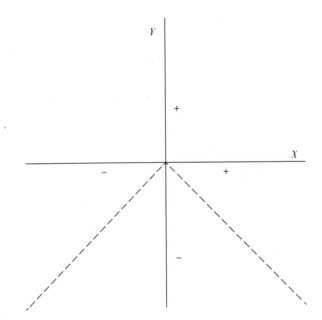

ABOUT THE AUTHOR

CARLO M. CIPOLLA (1922–2000) was an Italian economic historian, Fulbright Fellow, and professor at the University of California, Berkeley. Cipolla was elected as a Corresponding Fellow of the British Academy in 1989 and awarded the International Balzan Prize for Economic History in 1995. He also held honorary degrees in Italy and Switzerland.

His classic treatise *The Basic Laws of Human Stupidity* has sold more than half a million copies worldwide in more than ten languages.